The Handbook for Social Fitness

What is Social Fitness?

In our fast-paced and interconnected world, the significance of physical fitness is widely acknowledged, as individuals strive to maintain their bodily health through exercise and proper nutrition. However, there's another form of wellness that's just as crucial, yet often overlooked: social fitness. Social fitness encompasses the skills, behaviors, and attitudes necessary to navigate and thrive in our complex web of human relationships. Just as we sculpt our bodies to be strong and resilient, we can also cultivate our social aptitude to forge meaningful connections, resolve conflicts, and foster empathy in a world where interactions often extend beyond the confines of physical space.

Imagine a world where social interactions occur not only in face-to-face conversations but also across digital platforms and virtual realms. In this landscape, social fitness becomes an essential tool for building and maintaining relationships that transcend the boundaries of time and space. It's about effectively communicating our thoughts and emotions, understanding the perspectives of others, and resolving conflicts with empathy and grace. It's about navigating the intricate dance of friendships, family bonds, professional relationships, and even fleeting online connections.

Just like physical fitness requires regular exercise and mindful nutrition, social fitness demands intentional effort and ongoing practice. Developing social fitness involves honing essential skills such as active listening, clear communication, and emotional intelligence. It's about recognizing the impact of our words and actions on others and adjusting our behavior to foster positive interactions.

Social fitness empowers us to build a supportive community, whether it's within our close circles or across digital networks. It allows us to address conflicts constructively, turning challenges into opportunities for growth.

In the pages of this handbook, we'll delve into the intricacies of social fitness, exploring how to forge authentic connections, communicate effectively in both face-to-face and digital settings, and cultivate empathy even in a hyperconnected world. We'll learn to navigate conflicts with grace, set healthy boundaries in the digital realm, and build a resilient spirit that can weather the storms of social challenges. As our lives become increasingly intertwined with technology, we'll discuss strategies for mindful social media usage and the importance of fostering intergenerational connections.

Join us on this journey to understand, practice, and master the art of social fitness. Just as physical exercise enhances our bodies, cultivating social fitness will enhance our relationships, enrich our

lives, and help us navigate the
complexities of a rapidly evolving society.

Balancing Online and Offline Interactions: Navigating the Spectrum of Social Fitness

In the age of digital connectivity, our interactions span a vast spectrum that encompasses both online and offline realms. As we explore the concept of social fitness, it becomes evident that one of its fundamental aspects is the art of balancing these interactions. Striking the right equilibrium between our digital lives and our face-to-face engagements is crucial for nurturing meaningful relationships, fostering empathy, and maintaining our overall well-being.

The Dichotomy of Connection: On one hand, the digital age has granted us unparalleled opportunities to connect with individuals from across the globe, bridging geographical distances and fostering a sense of virtual community. Social media platforms, messaging apps, and online forums have allowed us to maintain connections, share experiences, and discover common interests in ways that were previously unimaginable. These digital tools have transformed the way we communicate and allowed us to be a part of each other's lives, regardless of physical proximity.

The Need for In-Person Connection: On the other hand, the virtual world cannot fully replicate the depth and richness of in-person interactions. The nuances of facial expressions, tone of voice, and body language convey a wealth of information that digital communication often lacks. Genuine, face-to-face interactions enable us to build a deeper level of understanding and empathy. They provide the context for laughter, tears, and shared experiences that shape our relationships and memories.

The Risk of Imbalance: However, an overreliance on digital communication at the expense of in-person connections can lead to a sense of isolation, superficial relationships, and a diminished ability to empathize with others. Spending excessive time online can inadvertently result in reduced social skills and an inability to navigate real-life social dynamics effectively. Conversely, neglecting our digital presence might isolate us from a world that thrives on virtual interaction and networking opportunities.

Strategies for Balance: Achieving a harmonious balance between online and offline interactions is a cornerstone of social fitness. Mindful technology use involves setting boundaries for screen time, designating tech-free moments, and choosing to engage in activities that encourage face-to-face connections. Regularly spending time with friends and loved ones in person helps nurture authentic relationships, while staying active in digital spaces ensures that we stay connected to the broader world and its ongoing conversations.

A Holistic Approach: The pursuit of social fitness, therefore, calls for a holistic approach that acknowledges the value of both online and offline interactions. It encourages us to be intentional in our digital presence, mindful in our communication, and proactive in creating opportunities for in-person connections. Striking this balance empowers us to experience the full spectrum of human interaction, allowing us to harness the strengths of both worlds while minimizing the risks of isolation and disconnection.

In the pages ahead, we'll explore practical strategies for achieving this balance, ensuring that our digital interactions enhance, rather than replace, the richness of our real-world connections. Through this exploration, we'll discover how social fitness equips us with the tools to thrive in the complex interplay of online and offline relationships, ultimately enriching our lives and the lives of those around us.

Understanding Social Fitness

In a world where connections are not only physical but also digital, mastering the art of social fitness becomes increasingly important. This chapter delves into the heart of social fitness, exploring its definition, the key components that contribute to social well-being, and the essential skills that form its foundation.

Defining Social Fitness: Navigating the Web of Relationships Social fitness is the dynamic and adaptive ability to engage in healthy relationships and interactions across a spectrum of contexts. It involves nurturing authentic connections, cultivating effective communication skills, and resolving conflicts constructively. Just as physical fitness empowers us to navigate various physical challenges, social fitness equips us with the skills and resilience needed to navigate the complex terrain of human relationships.

Components of Social Well-being: Building a Strong Foundation Social well-being comprises several interrelated components that collectively contribute to a fulfilled and meaningful life:

Emotional Connections: The quality and depth of our emotional connections are central to social fitness. Cultivating meaningful relationships, whether with family, friends, or colleagues, provides us with a support network that enhances our overall well-being. These connections are built on trust, empathy, and mutual understanding.

Communication Skills: Effective communication is the bedrock of successful relationships. It involves not only conveying thoughts and feelings clearly but also actively listening and interpreting the messages of others. Good communication fosters understanding, minimizes misunderstandings, and helps build rapport.

Empathy and Understanding: Empathy is the ability to step into another person's shoes and understand their thoughts, feelings, and perspectives. It's the foundation of compassion and forming connections that transcend surface interactions. Empathy facilitates genuine emotional bonds and enables us to respond sensitively to others' needs.

Conflict Resolution: Conflicts are inevitable in any relationship, but how we navigate them defines the health of those relationships. Social fitness includes the ability to manage conflicts constructively, addressing differences with respect and open-mindedness. Skillful conflict resolution transforms challenges into opportunities for growth and understanding.

Emotional Connections: The Power of Authentic Relationships Authentic emotional connections are at the core of social fitness. Nurturing these connections requires mutual vulnerability, trust, and shared experiences. Strong emotional bonds provide a sense of belonging, emotional support during tough times, and a platform for celebrating joys.

Communication Skills: The Art of Conveying and Listening Effective communication involves both expressing our thoughts and emotions clearly and genuinely, as well as being receptive to the messages of others. Active listening, where we engage with others' words and show empathy, is as important as articulating our own perspectives. It's the bridge that fosters understanding and deepens relationships.

Empathy and Understanding: Building Bridges of Compassion Empathy is the cornerstone of social fitness, allowing us to connect with others on a deeper level. It requires setting aside our biases and judgments, actively seeking to understand the feelings and experiences of others. Empathy builds bridges between diverse individuals and creates a sense of unity that transcends differences.

Conflict Resolution: Transforming Challenges into Growth Conflict is a natural part of relationships, and social fitness involves addressing conflicts with skill and grace. Constructive conflict resolution requires active listening, effective communication, and a willingness to compromise. When handled well, conflicts become opportunities to better understand each other and find common ground.

Building Meaningful Relationships

Relationships lie at the heart of human experience, shaping our lives in profound ways. This chapter explores the art of building and nurturing meaningful relationships across various contexts. From family bonds to professional networks, and even the digital realm, we'll uncover the dynamics of authentic connections and the importance of balancing depth and breadth.

The Power of Authentic Connections:

Beyond Surface Interactions Authentic

connections form the basis of fulfilling relationships. These connections are built on trust, mutual respect, and shared values. Authenticity involves showing vulnerability, expressing genuine emotions, and embracing imperfections. In a world where curated images and personas abound, cultivating authenticity fosters genuine bonds that stand the test of time.

Nurturing Friendships and Family Bonds: The Foundation of Social Support Friendships and family bonds are the cornerstones of our social support networks. Nurturing these relationships involves investing time, effort, and emotional energy. Quality time spent together, active listening, and being there for one another during both joyous and challenging moments solidify these bonds, creating a sense of belonging and security.

Cultivating Professional Relationships: Collaboration and Growth Professional relationships extend beyond mere networking; they are pathways to collaboration, mentorship, and personal growth. Building a strong professional network involves being genuine, demonstrating reliability, and offering assistance when needed. Cultivating these connections contributes to career development and provides opportunities for knowledge exchange.

Online Relationships: Balancing Depth and Breadth The digital age has expanded the reach of our relationships beyond geographical limitations. Online interactions offer the potential for diverse connections across cultures and backgrounds. While online platforms facilitate the exchange of ideas and the formation of global communities, it's essential to strike a balance between maintaining a broad network and nurturing deeper, more meaningful connections.

Balancing Depth and Breadth in Online Relationships: Finding the right balance between depth and breadth in online relationships is crucial. While broad connections provide exposure to different perspectives, investing time in cultivating a few deeper connections allows for more meaningful interactions. Engaging in thoughtful conversations, sharing experiences, and supporting one another can elevate digital interactions from superficial to substantial.

Mindful Digital Communication: In the digital realm, communication skills are paramount. Thoughtful communication involves respecting others' opinions, maintaining a positive tone, and being aware of the potential for misinterpretation due to the absence of nonverbal cues. Mindful digital communication fosters understanding and minimizes the risk of conflicts arising from misunderstandings.

Navigating Challenges of Online Relationships: Online relationships come with unique challenges, including maintaining privacy, managing time spent online, and addressing issues of authenticity and trust. It's important to be discerning about the information shared online and to prioritize offline interactions that provide a deeper sense of connection.

Fostering Offline Connections in a Digital Age: Balancing online relationships with face-to-face interactions is essential for social fitness. Actively seeking opportunities to meet online connections in person can enhance the depth of these relationships. In-person interactions provide a fuller understanding of the other person and create memories that strengthen the bond.

In the journey of building meaningful relationships, remember that authenticity, active engagement, and mindful communication are the driving forces that transform casual connections into lasting, enriching bonds. Whether within your family, among friends, within your professional circle, or in the vast digital landscape, cultivating these connections

enhances your social fitness and enriches
your life.

Communication Skills for Social Fitness

Effective communication serves as the backbone of successful relationships and plays a pivotal role in social fitness. This chapter explores the multifaceted aspects of communication skills, encompassing active listening techniques, the art of verbal and nonverbal communication, navigating digital communication etiquette, and overcoming barriers to clear understanding.

Active Listening Techniques: Fostering Understanding and Connection Active listening is the cornerstone of empathetic communication. It involves not only hearing the words being spoken but also understanding the emotions and intentions behind them. Practicing active listening means giving your full attention, asking clarifying questions, and demonstrating genuine interest. This technique enhances your understanding of others and strengthens the connection between you.

Effective Verbal and Nonverbal Communication: Conveying Messages Clearly Verbal communication is not solely about the words you choose; it also involves tone, pacing, and emphasis. Clear verbal communication requires using language that is precise and easy to understand. Additionally, nonverbal cues, such as body language and facial expressions, convey a wealth of information. Being aware of your nonverbal signals and interpreting those of others enhances the accuracy of your communication.

Digital Communication Etiquette: Navigating the Virtual Landscape In the era of digital interactions, proper communication etiquette is essential. Whether in emails, text messages, or social media posts, using polite language, observing cultural sensitivities, and considering the tone of your messages are vital. Emoticons, punctuation, and context become essential tools for conveying emotions accurately.

Overcoming Communication Barriers: Enhancing Clarity and Connection Effective communication faces various barriers, such as language differences, cognitive biases, and technological limitations. Overcoming these barriers involves practicing patience, actively seeking common ground, and using clear language. Being open to learning about others' communication styles and adapting your approach accordingly enhances your ability to connect across differences.

Cultivating Active Listening Skills: Developing active listening skills requires mindfulness and intentionality. Avoid interrupting, truly focus on the speaker, and respond thoughtfully. Clarifying questions, such as "Can you elaborate on that?" or "Could you share an example?"

encourage deeper conversations and signal that you value the speaker's perspective.

Mastering Verbal and Nonverbal Dynamics: Effective verbal communication involves using a conversational tone, avoiding jargon or complex language, and considering the pace of your speech. Nonverbal cues, such as maintaining eye contact, nodding, and using open body language, enhance the trust and understanding in your interactions.

Navigating the Digital Etiquette Landscape: When engaging in digital conversations, prioritize clarity over brevity. Use proper grammar and punctuation to avoid misunderstandings. Consider the recipient's cultural background and sensitivities, and remember that messages devoid of nonverbal cues might be interpreted differently than intended.

Breaking Down Communication Barriers: Overcoming communication barriers starts with acknowledging your own biases and working to understand others' perspectives. Use empathetic listening to uncover potential misinterpretations and clarify any points of confusion. Be patient when addressing language barriers and find common ground to bridge cultural differences.

In the pursuit of social fitness, honing your communication skills is paramount. These skills enable you to convey your thoughts effectively, empathize with others, and navigate various communication landscapes with finesse. By practicing active listening, refining verbal and nonverbal communication, adhering to digital communication etiquette, and overcoming barriers, you'll be well-equipped to engage in meaningful, impactful interactions that enhance your relationships and contribute to your overall social well-being.

Empathy and Emotional Intelligence

Empathy and emotional intelligence are the bedrock of social fitness, enabling us to connect deeply with others, understand their feelings, and navigate relationships with compassion and understanding. This chapter explores the concepts of empathy and emotional intelligence, delving into their significance in both digital and real-life interactions.

Understanding Empathy: The Heartbeat of Meaningful Connections
Empathy is the ability to place yourself in

another person's shoes, understanding their emotions, perspectives, and experiences. It involves recognizing and validating the feelings of others without judgment. Empathy fosters genuine connections, enhances trust, and creates an environment where people feel heard and valued.

Developing Emotional Intelligence: Nurturing Self-Awareness and Others Emotional intelligence (EQ) involves understanding and managing your own emotions as well as recognizing and responding to the emotions of others.

Cultivating emotional intelligence equips you with the tools to navigate social situations with sensitivity and tact. It involves being attuned to your emotions, understanding their impact on your interactions, and using this awareness to build healthier relationships.

Empathy in Digital Interactions: Navigating the Virtual Realm Empathy extends to the digital world, where the absence of physical cues poses unique challenges. Practicing digital empathy involves interpreting written words, recognizing underlying emotions, and responding with compassion. Digital empathy is about considering the feelings of others even when you can't see their faces or hear their tones.

Practicing Empathy in Everyday Life: Steps Toward Deeper Connections Empathy is a skill that can be developed and refined over time. Practicing empathy involves active listening, asking open-ended questions, and genuinely seeking to understand others' perspectives. Cultivating curiosity about others' experiences and emotions enhances your capacity for empathy.

Fostering Self-Empathy: Understanding Your Own Emotions Empathy begins with self-awareness. Acknowledge and validate your own emotions before extending empathy to others. By understanding your feelings, you're better equipped to relate to the experiences of others and respond with genuine compassion.

Cultivating Empathy Across Differences: Empathy transcends cultural, social, and personal differences. Recognize that everyone's experiences are valid, and seek to understand diverse perspectives. Learning about others' backgrounds and cultures fosters a broader understanding and connection.

Challenges and Benefits of Empathy: Empathy requires vulnerability and emotional labor, which can be challenging. However, the benefits far outweigh the difficulties. Empathy deepens relationships, reduces conflicts, and promotes a sense of belonging and mutual respect.

Digital Empathy: The Art of Virtual Compassion In digital interactions, strive to read between the lines, recognizing the emotions that may not be explicitly expressed. Respond with kindness, consideration, and patience, fostering a digital environment where empathy is the norm.

Incorporating empathy and emotional intelligence into your interactions enhances your ability to build strong, meaningful relationships. By understanding and valuing the feelings of others, practicing self-awareness, and cultivating empathy in both real-life and virtual settings, you contribute to your own social fitness and the well-being of those around you.

Conflict Resolution and Healthy Disagreements

Conflicts are an inevitable part of relationships, but how we handle them shapes the course of our connections. This chapter explores the intricacies of conflict resolution and the art of navigating disagreements with empathy and understanding, both in the physical and digital realms.

Types of Conflicts in Relationships: *Understanding the Spectrum* Conflicts manifest in various forms, from differing opinions and misunderstandings to deeper emotional clashes. Recognizing the types of conflicts—whether they're related to communication, values, or priorities—enables you to address them more effectively.

Strategies for Constructive Conflict Resolution: *Building Bridges, Not Barriers* Effective conflict resolution involves techniques that foster mutual understanding and growth. Active listening, reframing perspectives, and seeking common ground are essential tools. Embracing compromise, finding win-

win solutions, and using "I" statements instead of accusatory language create an atmosphere conducive to resolution.

Online Disagreements: *Maintaining Respectful Discourse in the Digital Age* Online platforms amplify disagreements due to the absence of nonverbal cues and the ease of anonymity. Engaging in online disagreements requires mindfulness, as words can be misinterpreted. Maintain respectful language, avoid personal attacks, and prioritize understanding over winning arguments.

Learning and Growing from Conflicts: ***Opportunities for Relationship Enhancement*** Conflicts, when navigated constructively, provide valuable opportunities for growth and connection. Rather than fearing conflicts, view them as chances to deepen your understanding of others and yourself. Reflect on the root causes of conflicts, and seek to understand the emotions and perspectives underlying them.

Healthy Disagreements: ***Navigating Tensions with Grace*** Practice active listening during disagreements, allowing each party to express their thoughts and feelings. Focus on the issue at hand rather than resorting to personal attacks. By maintaining open lines of communication, you create an environment where conflicts can be resolved with mutual respect.

Navigating Deep-Seated Conflicts: Some conflicts stem from deeper emotional triggers or long-standing issues. In such cases, it's important to address underlying concerns rather than merely addressing the surface disagreement. Acknowledge past experiences and emotions that contribute to the conflict, and work together to find healing and resolution.

Building Bridges through Compromise: Constructive conflict resolution often involves finding middle ground. Compromise requires flexibility and a willingness to meet halfway. By valuing the relationship and focusing on shared goals, you can collaboratively craft solutions that address both parties' needs.

Turning Conflicts into Opportunities for Growth: View conflicts as learning experiences. After a conflict, take time to reflect on what you've learned about yourself and the other person. Engage in open discussions about the conflict's root causes and brainstorm strategies to prevent similar conflicts in the future.

Online Disagreements: *Constructive Virtual Discourse* When engaging in online disagreements, approach the conversation with curiosity rather than aggression. Focus on understanding the other person's viewpoint, and avoid making assumptions. Be aware that written words can lack context, leading to misunderstandings.

Incorporating conflict resolution skills into your social fitness toolkit empowers you to navigate disagreements with grace and empathy. By recognizing the types of conflicts, applying strategies for resolution, maintaining respectful discourse online, and viewing conflicts as opportunities for growth, you foster a space where relationships flourish even in the face of challenges.

Navigating Social Media Mindfully

In an era of constant connectivity, achieving balance between our digital lives and real-world interactions is essential for social fitness. This chapter explores the challenges of digital overload, strategies for setting healthy boundaries, the importance of digital detox, and the value of nurturing genuine, offline experiences.

Recognizing Digital Overload: *The Impact on Social Well-being* Digital overload refers to the overwhelming influx of information, notifications, and interactions from various digital platforms. This overload can lead to increased stress, reduced focus, and strained relationships. Recognizing the signs of digital overload empowers you to take proactive steps toward balance.

Setting Healthy Boundaries: *Prioritizing Meaningful Connections* Boundaries are crucial for maintaining a healthy balance between your online and offline worlds. Establishing clear limits on screen time, defining when and where you engage with technology, and determining when to disconnect to focus on real-life interactions contribute to your overall well-being.

Digital Detox and Mindful Technology Use: *Reclaiming Present Moments* Taking regular breaks from digital devices through a digital detox can be revitalizing. Unplugging allows you to reconnect with yourself and your surroundings. Mindful technology use involves being intentional about your interactions online, being present in the moment, and choosing when to engage with technology.

Fostering Real-Life Experiences: *Nurturing Tangible Connections* While digital interactions offer convenience, nothing can replace the richness of face-to-face experiences. Prioritize spending quality time with loved ones, engaging in hobbies, and participating in activities that enhance your overall well-being. These experiences provide a sense of fulfillment that goes beyond the virtual world.

Balancing Online and Offline Engagement: Strive for a balanced engagement with both online and offline interactions. Dedicate time to connect with friends, family, and colleagues in person. Create opportunities for engaging in activities that allow you to be fully present, without the distractions of digital devices.

Creating Screen-Free Zones and Times: Designate specific areas and times as screen-free zones. This allows you to focus on interactions, self-care, and relaxation without the constant pull of digital notifications. These intentional breaks contribute to a healthier relationship with technology.

The Art of Digital Detox: *Restoring Mind-Body Harmony* Regular digital detoxes involve intentionally disconnecting from technology for a defined period. Engage in activities that nurture your mind and body, such as reading, exercising, or spending time in nature. The temporary break from screens allows you to recharge and return to digital interactions with renewed energy.

Integrating Mindful Technology Use:
When using technology, do so mindfully. Set specific goals for your digital interactions and use technology as a tool rather than a distraction. Avoid multitasking and focus on one activity at a time. Mindful technology use enhances your ability to engage deeply with both digital and real-world experiences.

The Balance between Digital and Analog: Striking the right balance between digital and analog experiences is a continuous journey. Regularly assess your screen time and its impact on your well-being. Adjust your habits as needed to ensure that your interactions online enhance rather than hinder your ability to connect with others and live a fulfilling life.

By recognizing digital overload, setting boundaries, embracing digital detox, and fostering real-life experiences, you can achieve a harmonious balance between the digital and analog aspects of your life. Balancing your engagement with technology ensures that your social fitness thrives, allowing you to connect deeply with others while savoring the richness of

genuine, in-person interactions.

Cultivating a Supportive Community

A supportive community plays a pivotal role in enhancing social fitness, providing a network of connections that foster empathy, understanding, and a sense of belonging. This chapter explores the significance of community, guiding you through finding like-minded groups, supporting social initiatives, and creating an environment that nurtures a strong sense of belonging.

The Role of Community in Social Fitness: *Nurturing Connections* Communities offer a sense of belonging, validation, and support. They create spaces where individuals can share experiences, seek advice, and engage in meaningful interactions. Cultivating a supportive community enhances social well-being by fostering connections that go beyond superficial interactions.

Finding Like-Minded Groups and Activities: *Shared Interests and Passions* Identify your interests and passions, then seek out groups or activities that align with them. Whether it's a book club, hiking group, or volunteering opportunity, shared interests form the foundation of meaningful connections. Engaging in activities you enjoy facilitates natural, authentic interactions.

Supporting Causes and Social Initiatives: *Contributing to a Larger Purpose* Engaging with causes and initiatives that resonate with your values enables you to connect with individuals who share your passion for positive change. Collaborating on projects, volunteering, or supporting social campaigns deepens your connections while making a meaningful impact.

Creating a Sense of Belonging: *Inclusivity and Mutual Support* Foster a sense of belonging by creating an inclusive and supportive environment within your community. Actively welcome new members, value diverse perspectives, and encourage open dialogue. Providing mutual support and celebrating each other's achievements cultivates a strong sense of unity.

Mindful Community Engagement: *Quality Over Quantity* Prioritize the quality of your interactions within a community over the quantity of connections. Engage authentically, contribute meaningfully, and take the time to build relationships that resonate on a deeper level.

Balancing Online and Offline Community Engagement: While online communities offer convenience, in-person interactions provide a depth that virtual interactions often lack. Strive for a balance between online and offline engagement, aiming to meet members of your community in person when possible.

Fostering Supportive Relationships: Build supportive relationships within your community by actively listening, offering assistance, and celebrating each other's successes. Engaging in meaningful conversations and showing empathy fosters a sense of trust and mutual understanding.

Embracing Vulnerability and Authenticity: Create an atmosphere where vulnerability and authenticity are valued. Sharing your own experiences and challenges encourages others to open up as well, deepening the connections within your community.

The Power of Shared Goals and Values: Communities that share common goals and values have a stronger sense of purpose and unity. Engage in discussions about shared values and collaborate on projects that align with these values to foster a deep sense of connection.

By actively seeking out like-minded groups, supporting social initiatives, and creating an inclusive sense of belonging within your community, you contribute to your own social fitness while enriching the lives of those around you. Cultivating a supportive community enhances your capacity for empathy, understanding, and meaningful connections, ultimately enhancing your overall social well-being.

Building Resilience and Coping Skills

Resilience and coping skills are essential components of social fitness, equipping you with the ability to navigate challenges, cope with setbacks, and maintain your well-being in the face of adversity. This chapter delves into strategies for dealing with social rejection, handling cyberbullying and online harassment, developing resilience in the digital world, and recognizing when to seek help.

Dealing with Social Rejection: *A Path to Resilience* Social rejection is a universal experience, but it's how you respond that shapes your resilience. Remember that rejection doesn't define your worth. Focus on your strengths, surround yourself with supportive individuals, and engage in activities that uplift your spirits.

Handling Cyberbullying and Online Harassment: *Empowerment through Action* Online interactions can sometimes turn negative, resulting in cyberbullying and harassment. Responding to such situations requires strength and empowerment. Document the evidence, block or report the offenders, and seek support from friends, family, or appropriate authorities.

Developing Resilience in the Face of Online Challenges: Resilience involves bouncing back from adversity and growing stronger as a result. Cultivate a growth mindset by viewing challenges as opportunities for growth. Practice self-compassion, maintain a support network, and engage in activities that boost your emotional well-being.

Recognizing When to Seek Help: *Prioritizing Mental Health* Sometimes, challenges may become overwhelming, affecting your mental well-being. It's important to recognize when you need professional help. Reach out to mental health professionals, counselors, or therapists who can provide guidance and support.

Cultivating Self-Compassion: *Treating Yourself with Kindness* Practice self-compassion by treating yourself as you would a close friend. Be understanding and patient with yourself when facing difficulties. Acknowledge your emotions without judgment and remember that setbacks are a natural part of growth.

Fostering a Supportive Network: *Surrounding Yourself with Positivity* Build a network of supportive friends and family who uplift and encourage you. These individuals can provide comfort, advice, and perspective during challenging times.

Building Emotional Regulation Skills: *Managing Reactions* Develop emotional regulation skills to manage your reactions in difficult situations. Practice mindfulness, deep breathing, and grounding techniques to center yourself when faced with stressors.

Empowering Responses to Cyberbullying: Respond to cyberbullying with empowerment rather than succumbing to negativity. Focus on positivity, share your experiences with trusted individuals, and engage in activities that remind you of your strengths and value.

Seeking Growth and Learning from Challenges: View challenges as opportunities for growth and learning. Embrace setbacks as stepping stones toward a stronger, more resilient version of yourself. By facing difficulties head-on, you cultivate resilience and enhance your coping skills.

The Importance of Self-Care in Resilience: Prioritize self-care as an integral part of building resilience. Engage in activities that bring you joy, relaxation, and peace. These practices bolster your emotional well-being, providing a foundation for navigating challenges.

As you navigate social rejection, handle online challenges, and build resilience, remember that your ability to cope with adversity strengthens your social fitness. By developing resilience, practicing self-compassion, fostering a supportive network, and seeking help when needed, you empower yourself to overcome obstacles, enhance your emotional well-being, and maintain healthy, positive relationships both in person and online.

Fostering Intergenerational Connections

Intergenerational connections provide a unique opportunity to enrich your social fitness by bridging gaps, sharing wisdom, and learning from diverse age groups. This chapter explores the value of intergenerational relationships, guiding you through ways to bridge the generation gap, share experiences, gain insights, and create bonds that span across different ages.

Bridging the Generation Gap: *Embracing Diversity* Generational differences can lead to misunderstandings, but they also offer rich opportunities for growth. Embrace the diversity of perspectives, values, and experiences that different age groups bring to the table.

Sharing Wisdom and Experiences: *The Gift of Stories* Each generation has its own set of experiences and stories that hold invaluable lessons. Engage in conversations with older individuals to learn from their life journeys and share your own experiences, passing on insights to younger generations.

Learning from Different Age Groups: *A Two-Way Exchange* Intergenerational connections are a two-way street. While older individuals can offer wisdom and guidance, younger generations bring fresh perspectives and innovative ideas. Be open to learning from one another, fostering mutual growth.

Creating Multi-Generational Bonds: *Building Lasting Relationships* Seek out opportunities to connect with people of different age groups. Engage in activities, events, and groups that encourage intergenerational interactions. Create a space where conversations flow naturally, leading to meaningful relationships.

Cultivating Empathy Across Generations: Empathy is essential for understanding the experiences of different generations. Put yourself in others' shoes, listen actively, and ask questions to uncover their perspectives. This builds bridges and strengthens connections.

Breaking Stereotypes and Prejudices:
Generational stereotypes and prejudices can hinder meaningful connections. Challenge assumptions by engaging in conversations that reveal the unique qualities, experiences, and aspirations of each age group.

Sharing Traditions and Cultural Heritage: Interacting with individuals from different generations offers an opportunity to share and celebrate cultural traditions. Learning about each other's customs fosters mutual respect and understanding.

Creating an Intergenerational Support Network: Intergenerational connections create a support network that transcends age. Older individuals can offer advice and guidance, while younger generations provide assistance with technology and contemporary trends.

Engaging in Mentorship and Learning Opportunities: Mentorship across generations benefits both parties. Older individuals can provide guidance and mentorship to younger ones, while younger generations can share insights into emerging technologies and trends.

Sustaining Intergenerational Bonds: Nurturing intergenerational connections requires consistent effort. Regularly engage in conversations, attend intergenerational events, and celebrate milestones together. These actions foster lasting relationships that continue to evolve over time.

By fostering intergenerational connections, you enrich your social fitness through a diverse range of perspectives, experiences, and insights. Bridging the generation gap, sharing wisdom, learning from different age groups, and creating bonds that transcend time contribute to a deeper understanding of the world and the people in it. Intergenerational relationships enhance your ability to connect with others on a meaningful level, contributing to your overall social well-being.

Future Trends in Social Fitness

The landscape of social fitness is constantly evolving, shaped by technological advancements, changing social dynamics, and emerging trends. This chapter delves into the future of social fitness, exploring how technological innovations influence social interaction, how relationships continue to evolve, and how you can prepare for the shifting dynamics of tomorrow.

Technological Innovations and Social Interaction: *A Dynamic Relationship*

As technology continues to advance, its impact on social interaction becomes more profound. Virtual reality, augmented reality, and artificial intelligence are transforming how we connect, enabling immersive experiences that bridge physical and digital worlds. Embrace these innovations to enhance your social fitness through new modes of interaction and connection.

Shaping the Evolution of Social Relationships: *Adapting to Change*

Social relationships are undergoing a metamorphosis due to technological changes. Online connections are becoming more integral to our lives, supplementing offline interactions. Developing the flexibility to adapt to these evolving dynamics is essential for maintaining a robust social fitness.

Preparing for Changing Social Dynamics: *Flexibility and Openness* Anticipate that the nature of social interactions will continue to shift. Be open to forming connections across distances, engaging in virtual communities, and embracing new norms of digital communication. The ability to navigate both physical and virtual interactions seamlessly will be a hallmark of future social fitness.

The Role of Digital Empathy and Mindful Engagement: As technological interactions become more prevalent, the importance of digital empathy and mindful engagement will increase. Understanding the nuances of digital communication, interpreting emotions through text, and fostering positive online interactions will be crucial for maintaining healthy relationships.

Balancing Virtual and Physical Worlds: Striking a balance between virtual and physical interactions will be an ongoing challenge. Prioritize face-to-face engagements when possible to maintain the depth of human connections, while also leveraging digital platforms to foster global connections and access diverse perspectives.

Enhancing Relationships Through Technology: Leverage technology to enhance your relationships. Virtual meetups, collaborative projects, and shared online experiences can deepen connections and bridge geographical barriers. However, remember that genuine, in-person interactions remain irreplaceable.

Embracing Continuous Learning and Adaptation: Future trends in social fitness demand a commitment to continuous learning and adaptation. Stay informed about emerging technologies, trends in communication, and evolving social norms. Embrace a growth mindset that enables you to thrive in a changing social landscape.

Navigating Ethical and Privacy Considerations: As technology evolves, ethical and privacy concerns become more complex. Educate yourself about the ethical use of technology, digital privacy, and data security. Make informed choices that align with your values and protect your well-being.

Maintaining Authenticity Amid Technological Advancements: In the face of technological changes, authenticity remains a cornerstone of social fitness. Embrace technology as a tool to enhance, rather than replace, genuine human interactions. Strive to convey your true self in both digital and physical interactions.

Cultivating Resilience in the Face of Change: Adapting to future trends in social fitness requires resilience. Embrace change with an open mind, view challenges as learning opportunities, and focus on building strong relationships that withstand the test of time and technological shifts.

By understanding and embracing the future trends in social fitness, you position yourself to thrive in an ever-evolving world. Prepare to navigate the integration of technology, the shaping of social relationships, and the changing dynamics of human interaction with flexibility, empathy, and an unwavering commitment to authentic and meaningful connections.

Conclusion

As you've journeyed through the various facets of social fitness, you've uncovered the intricacies of building and nurturing meaningful connections, both in person and in the digital realm. This concluding chapter encapsulates the essence of your exploration, emphasizing the ongoing nature of your social fitness journey, the importance of embracing change and growth, and providing resources for further exploration.

The Continual Journey of Social Fitness: Social fitness is not a destination but an ongoing journey. It's a dynamic process that involves continuous learning, growth, and adaptation. Just as physical fitness requires consistent effort, nurturing your social well-being demands mindfulness, intentionality, and a willingness to explore new approaches.

Embracing Change and Growth: Change is a constant companion in life, shaping our relationships, interactions, and perspectives. Embrace change as an opportunity for growth rather than a hurdle to overcome. Through each challenge, setback, or advancement, your ability to adapt and evolve contributes to your overall social fitness.

Reflecting on Your Progress: Take a moment to reflect on the insights you've gained and the strategies you've learned throughout this handbook. Consider the areas where you've already excelled in nurturing your social well-being, as well as those where you see opportunities for further growth.

Resources for Further Exploration: The journey of social fitness is enriched by continuous learning and exploration. Here are some resources to aid you on your path:

- ***Books:*** Dive deeper into the topics covered in this handbook through recommended books on communication, empathy, resilience, and personal development.

- ***Online Courses:*** Explore online courses that focus on interpersonal skills, emotional intelligence, and building meaningful relationships.

- ***Workshops and Seminars:*** Participate in local workshops and seminars that provide hands-on guidance for enhancing your social fitness.

Support Groups: Join local or online support groups to connect with others who are also working on their social well-being.

Professional Support: If you find yourself facing significant challenges, consider seeking support from therapists, counselors, or life coaches.

Mindfulness and Meditation: Explore mindfulness practices and meditation techniques that promote emotional regulation and self-awareness.

Celebrating Your Journey: Remember that every step you take toward improving your social fitness is an achievement worth celebrating. Each connection you foster, each interaction you engage in mindfully, and each challenge you navigate contributes to your overall well-being and the well-being of those around you.

A Future of Connectedness: As you conclude this handbook, carry forward the insights and strategies you've gained to navigate the evolving landscape of social fitness. Embrace the future with a sense of excitement, curiosity, and the knowledge that your journey toward deeper connections and enhanced well-being continues to unfold.

Social fitness is not a solitary endeavor but a collective journey that impacts not only your life but also the lives of those you connect with. May your pursuit of social well-being lead you to a future filled with meaningful relationships, personal growth, and a deep sense of fulfillment.

About the Author

Antonio is a father of two children who he loves dearly. He has been working in the field of education for almost twenty-five years, primarily with students ages K-21. He believes that basic education is the key to supporting more people all over the world. As we enter into the digital age, it has become obvious that making meaningful relationships in this world is not only difficult to do, but necessary and vital for humanity's continued success. It is his hope that one day, everyone will read this handbook and become stronger at cultivating more meaningful relationships. Education is truly the most powerful tool we have to transform the future.

Disclaimer

Please note that the advice provided is intended for informational purposes only and should not be taken as legal or professional advice. It is important to always seek the guidance of a qualified professional when making decisions that may have legal consequences. Additionally, it is important to use your own judgment and intuition when making any decisions, as ultimately you are responsible for the outcome. Please consult with a qualified professional before making any decisions that may have legal or other significant consequences. This disclaimer is not intended to limit or exclude any liability that may not be excluded or limited by law.

This handbook was a collaboration between the author and an open AI platform, with the sole purpose of enriching everyone all over the world with more meaningful relationships.

First Edition: 2023
ISBN: 9798858035640

Content Feedback: Please direct all feedback to **www.handbooksforhumanity.com**

Copyright © 2023

Gufo Publishing